Newbridge Discovery Links®

For a Good Cause

Patricia Baehr

Newbridge

A Haights Cross Communications ◀ Company

For a Good Cause
ISBN: 1-58273-725-8

Program Author: Dr. Brenda Parkes, Literacy Expert
Content Reviewers: Portasue Andary, Paws With A Cause, Wayland, MI;
  Cindy Burstein, City of Philadelphia Mural Arts Program, Philadelphia, PA;
  Jake Scott, National Wildlife Federation, Naples, FL
Teacher Reviewer: Denise Ott, Olmsted 67, Buffalo, NY

Written by Patricia Baehr
Editorial and Design Assistance by Curriculum Concepts

Newbridge Educational Publishing
333 East 38th Street, New York, NY 10016
www.newbridgeonline.com

Cover Photograph: Mural painters at work
Table of Contents Photograph: A detail from the mural called "The Peace Wall"

Photo Credits:
Cover: Jack Ramsdale; Contents page: "The Peace Wall" by Jane Golden and Peter Pagast, 29th and
Wharton Streets, Funding provided by the William Penn Foundation, photograph by Jack Ramsdale;
pages 4–5: A. Ramey/PhotoEdit; pages 6–7: David Young-Wolff/PhotoEdit; pages 8–9: (background) Kevin
Fleming/CORBIS; page 9: (inset) Farley Lewis/Photo Researchers, Inc.; page 10: Ted Levin/Animals
Animals/Earth Scenes; page 11: Karl H. Switak/Photo Researchers, Inc.; page 12: (top) John Pontier/
Animals Animals/Earth Scenes, (bottom) Courtesy of Young Friends of the Everglades; page 13: Stevan
Stefanovic/OKAPIA/Photo Researchers, Inc.; page 14: Daniel J. Cox/Natural Exposures; page 16–17: "The
Peace Wall" by Jane Golden and Peter Pagast, 29th and Wharton Streets, Funding provided by the William
Penn Foundation, photograph by Jack Ramsdale; page 18: (top) Jack Ramsdale, (bottom) "The Peace Wall"
by Jane Golden and Peter Pagast, 29th and Wharton Streets, Funding provided by the William Penn
Foundation, photograph by Jack Ramsdale; page 19: (background) Wild Iris, 34th and Wallace, by Paul
Santolen, Funded by Philadelphia Museum of Art & the City of Philadelphia, photo by Jack Ramsdale,
(inset) Paul Robeson by Peter Pagast, 4502 Chestnut Street, Funded by University City District/Sovereign
Bank; page 20: (background) "Choices" by Cavin Jones, photo by Jack Ramsdale, (inset) Community
Leaders, 21st and Dauphin Streets, Funding provided by the William Penn Foundation Project of the Big
Picture Program of MAP; page 21: (background) Community Leaders, 21st and Dauphin Streets, Funding
provided by the William Penn Foundation Project of the Big Picture Program of MAP, (inset) History of
Neighborhood (in progress), 1039 Spring Garden Street; pages 22–23: Lawrence Migdale/Photo
Researchers, Inc.; page 24: A. Ramey/ Stock Boston; page 25: (left) Bonnie Kamin/ PhotoEdit, (right)
Gayna Hoffman/Stock Boston; page 26: (top) Courtesy of Paws With A Cause, (bottom) Frank
Siteman/Stock Boston; page 27: Grantpix/Photo Researchers, Inc.; page 28: Photo Researchers, Inc.; page
29: Frank Siteman/Stock Boston; page 30: David Young-Wolff/PhotoEdit

Map page 15: From the book *The Everglades: River of Grass, 50th Anniversary Edition*, copyright © 1997 by
Marjory Stoneman Douglas. Used by permission of Pineapple Press. Inc.

10 9 8 7 6 5 4 3 2

Table of Contents

A Helping Hand

Many of us would like to make the world a better place, but what can we do? How much can one person accomplish? Luckily, some people don't stop to wonder. They act!

Millard and Linda Fuller believed that every family should have the opportunity to own a home. Their goal was to build new houses and fix up old ones. They liked the idea of having **volunteers** and new home owners work together, so people could help build their own homes. So, in 1976, they created Habitat for Humanity in Americus, Georgia.

Over the next several years, more and more people volunteered for Habitat for Humanity, and it spread to other states and countries.

Volunteers for Habitat for Humanity are in the process of putting up a frame of a new house in Los Angeles, California.

Jimmy Carter (right) lends a hand to Habitat for Humanity home owners and volunteers.

In 1984, former U.S. President Jimmy Carter and his wife, Rosalynn, showed interest in Habitat and gave volunteers in Americus a helping hand. Since then, the Carters have volunteered for Habitat at least one week each year.

Families who receive homes begin by filling out an application. They are chosen according to their need. They also must agree to pay back a loan and work at least 300 hours with Habitat, helping to build homes for others.

Many children also volunteer for the organization. They help plant trees and gardens, or clear debris from construction sites. They paint, serve meals to other volunteers, and work on Habitat web pages and newsletters.

College students participate in construction during school breaks, and even the youngest volunteers help out by making welcome baskets for new home owners.

Today, the organization the Fullers began in Americus operates in 64 countries around the world and has built more than 100,000 homes.

In the beginning, efforts like these may touch only one life or one small part of a community. But, often, results ripple out like rings around a pebble that has been tossed into a lake. In this book you will read about other programs that also began small and grew to make a difference in many people's lives.

This is the same house shown on page 5. You can see that it is now almost completely finished, thanks to the help of so many Habitat volunteers.

River of Grass

Every year, close to a million people come to the Everglades in South Florida. It is a place unlike anywhere else on Earth. The Everglades is home to hundreds of different plants and animals, many of which are found nowhere else in the world. But if it wasn't for the determination and vision of one woman, this amazing place might have disappeared.

Many people wanted to help Florida grow by using parts of the Everglades and the land around it for new homes, businesses, and farms. But a newspaper reporter named Marjory Stoneman Douglas had been studying the area. In a book first published in 1947 called *The Everglades: River of Grass*, she made people aware of the importance of these **wetlands** to Florida's plant and animal life, as well as to its water supply. As a result, the U.S. government **preserved** part of the Everglades as a national park.

Marjory Stoneman Douglas with the saw grass of the Everglades. Saw grass grows side by side with many other plants and trees in the Everglades.

The spoonbill uses its spoon-shaped bill to scoop up frogs, small fish, and shellfish. The Everglades is one of the spoonbills' most important habitats in North America.

Then, in 1969, a new jetport was proposed for southern Florida. Designed to cover 39 square miles, the jetport would have stopped the flow of water across the Everglades. Marjory Stoneman Douglas was ready to speak out again. She also realized that an organization would be more effective than the efforts of any individual. So she created Friends of the Everglades. She and other members of Friends traveled the state tirelessly, giving speeches and making people aware of the importance of saving the Everglades. Thanks to their combined efforts, the plans for a jetport were dropped. However, even without the jetport, the Everglades remained endangered, so Douglas and the Friends of the Everglades continued their work. For the next ten years, Douglas wrote a column about conservation for a newsletter published by Friends of the Everglades. She also served as president of the organization until 1991.

Since the start of Friends, some types of pollution have been reduced. Hundreds of thousands of acres have been added to the Everglades National Park and surrounding preserved areas. Friends of the Everglades also educates the public about environmental issues, and works hard to get laws passed that will protect this important **ecosystem**. When Hurricane Andrew blew through the Everglades in 1992, Friends volunteers were there cleaning up the damage.

A few years later, the Friends were called upon again to save the Everglades from further **destruction**.

Snakes in the Everglades, such as this Florida banded water snake, have adapted to survive in and around water.

Alligators dig deep holes that collect water. These are called gator holes and are used by many plants and animals in the Everglades.

In 1994, there was talk that developers wanted to build a sports/entertainment theme park in an area near the Everglades. It had been almost 25 years since Douglas first started her organization. Now, she inspired a new generation to take up the cause. Teachers and students at Howard Drive Elementary School in Miami, Florida, formed a new organization called Young Friends of the Everglades.

The two groups' educational projects about the environment helped people understand the importance of leaving areas around the Everglades undeveloped. Douglas, then 104 years old, was pleased. She said, "The children are our future, and we can't do without that!"

There are more than 6,000 active members of Friends of the Everglades and Young Friends of the Everglades.

The Everglades is a living, evolving ecosystem that is always changing. For the people of Florida, it is a constant challenge to balance the needs of the surrounding growing communities with those of such a delicate, wild area. The Everglades is not yet out of danger. Half of the original Everglades has been drained and made into farmland or paved over for roads. **Wading** birds have declined by 93 percent over the last 70 years, and many species of animals there are endangered or threatened.

Marjory Stoneman Douglas died in 1998, at the age of 108. At her request, her ashes were scattered over the wetlands she so loved. Friends of the Everglades and Young Friends of the Everglades remain committed to preserving this special place.

About a million people visit the Everglades National Park each year to enjoy its beauty, unusual plants, and animals.

Great egrets build a nest, bringing a new generation to the Everglades. Once close to **extinction**, they are now increasing in numbers.

More About

The Everglades

Marjory Stoneman Douglas wrote in her book, "There are no other Everglades in the world."

Besides being the largest wetland in the United States, the Everglades is unique in many other ways. The river that flows from Lake Okeechobee to the south coast of Florida is what Douglas called the River of Grass. It is a very slow-moving river, flowing downhill only a few inches per mile. Most rivers flow quickly, and run downhill hundreds of feet. Because the Everglades water moves so slowly, nutrients have time to soak into the soil, and plants have a chance to grow.

You can walk a mile in the Everglades and go through six different ecosystems. You can find fresh wetland consisting mainly of saw grass, subtropical tree islands with oak, hickory, palm, and mangrove trees around the coastline, wet prairies, drier upland pine forests, and cypress swamps.

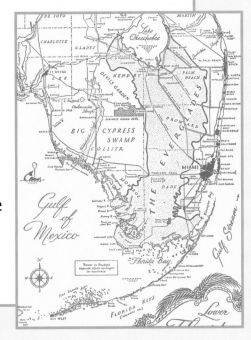

Painting a City

I magine a work of art as big as a three-story row house. Now imagine almost 2,000 of them! That's what one program in Philadelphia, Pennsylvania, has created. It is called the Mural Arts Program (MAP), and it has people painting more than 100 murals a year. They paint them on the sides of buildings that are from one to eight stories high. Each mural is large enough for a whole neighborhood to enjoy. The program, which started small, has now made Philadelphia the mural capital of the United States.

A photograph of neighbors joining hands inspired this mural called "The Peace Wall."

Over 10,000 young people have been involved with MAP, painting murals and attending workshops.

Jane Golden was one of the **founders** of the program, begun in 1984 as part of an effort to clean up the city. She had been painting murals in Los Angeles, and started a mural program there. She moved back east, and began working with a similar program in Philadelphia. Within just a few years, thousands of young people were participating, and in 1996 The Philadelphia Department of Recreation Mural Arts Program (MAP) was formed. MAP's mission is to work with community members to bring art and art education into their neighborhoods. Now MAP gets about a hundred requests a year to paint murals around the city. Local youth **participate**, and many local artists share their skills and ideas.

Jane Golden is the artistic director of MAP. She creates murals for it as well. Here she is working on the "Peace Wall" mural.

The murals show themes and subjects that are important to the neighborhoods in which they are painted.

Often, local people are the ones coming up with the ideas for the murals. A combination of students, parents, artists, other neighborhood residents, and public and private organizations all participate in their creation. They discuss the design and subject of each mural. People also participate by painting, sharing photographs for ideas, offering storage space for supplies, and even posing as models.

As a result, each mural not only brings a large work of art into the community, but it also creates a great amount of activity, cooperation, and pride.

{ Cavin Jones (inset) designed this mural, called "Choices." What types of activities are the people in the mural doing?

Cavin Jones is one of the local artists who has created beautiful murals for the program. Jones grew up in north Philadelphia. When he was a child he showed his talents, drawing on his street with chalk or a piece of broken brick. He studied art in college and became even more skilled as an artist. Now he enjoys getting his artwork out where it can be enjoyed by the community. Jones's ideas for his murals are presented to each neighborhood first, before the work begins.

More About

Painting a City

How do you create a mural?

One way is to make a grid of vertical and horizontal lines over a drawing. Each box of the grid is painted. Then a larger grid is drawn on the wall where the mural will go. Those boxes are painted to match the smaller example.

Another way is to project a slide onto the wall. That image is used as a guide for colors and shapes. A third technique, the stencil method, uses holes in paper that follow the artwork. The paper is then placed on the wall, and chalk is sprinkled over the holes. When the paper is removed, the chalk shows the outline of the drawing.

Years ago, the murals were painted with house paint. Time and weather caused some of the original murals to fade. Now a special paint is used. It has very bright colors and lasts longer under the hot sun.

Dependable Dogs

There are many things that people need to do every day, whether it's getting from place to place, opening doors, answering the phone, or eating. But because of a disability, some people can't do all of these things alone. You may have seen Guide Dogs helping people who can't see. But did you know that there are people with other kinds of disabilities who also use the help of **Assistance Dogs**? Find out who these dogs team up with, and how they are trained to help people get through their days.

A young boy and his dog take a walk. In what ways do you think the dog helps him?

{ This is graduation day for these dogs that are now ready to be Service Dogs.

Take a walk around Grand Rapids, Michigan, and you might see a puppy wearing a bright blue jacket. Jackets identify all the Assistance Dogs trained by Paws With A Cause when they are out in public. Their Hearing Dogs help people who are hard-of-hearing or deaf, and their Service Dogs help those with physical disabilities such as muscular dystrophy, cerebral palsy, and spinal cord injuries. Most Hearing Dogs are small and come from animal shelters. Large dogs are preferred as Service Dogs because of the physical tasks they must perform.

The PAWS story began with Michael Sapp, a truck driver, who trained dogs as a hobby. One of the people on his truck

route asked him to train his dog Crystal, a cairn terrier, to be a Hearing Dog. It was 1979, and at the time most dog training schools trained Guide Dogs to help the blind.

Sapp agreed, and was successful. After just a few weeks, friends of Crystal's family asked Sapp to train their dogs to be Hearing Dogs, too. He trained these dogs to **alert** deaf and hard-of-hearing people to important sounds, such as alarm clocks and smoke detectors.

At first, dogs were trained in their owners' homes. Now, PAWS trains all the dogs at its Michigan headquarters. Volunteers join the cause by raising the puppies in loving homes.

In these homes the puppies must learn to behave in all kinds of situations. Along with learning basic commands—like sit, down, stay, and come—they are taught not to chase other animals.

Then, after about a year, the puppies leave these homes and live at PAWS where they begin formal training. There they learn to respond to sounds and understand some sign language. After 200 hours of training they know how to alert their owner if the phone or doorbell rings, if an alarm clock goes off, or if a baby is crying.

The PAWS puppies are taken to many places, so they get used to being out in public.

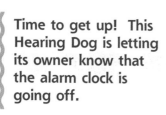

Time to get up! This Hearing Dog is letting its owner know that the alarm clock is going off.

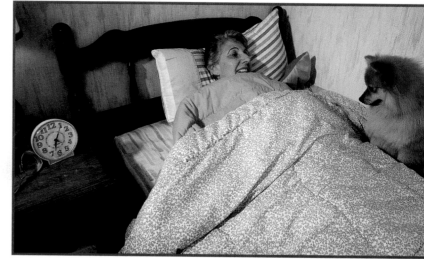

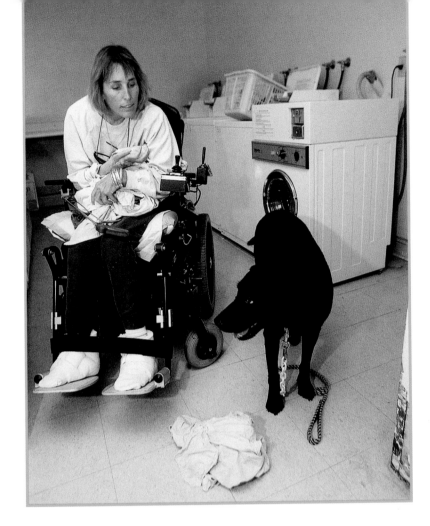

This woman's Service Dog helps her retrieve items from the floor.

Besides Paws With A Cause, there are now many other Service Dog organizations. For most of them, any breed of dog will do. However, they must be gentle animals, with the necessary physical strength, patience, and intelligence to do their jobs. They learn to behave well in public places such as libraries, museums, and doctors' offices.

All Service Dogs go through many hours of training to do various tasks. They learn to open doors, pull wheelchairs, turn light switches on and off, and pick up or retrieve items. All of these things help people perform their daily activities.

More About

Dependable Dogs

Many people with disabilities are more independent now, thanks to the different places which train dogs as **companion** animals. But not all of them have a disability that can be seen. Some people who team up with Service Dogs have heart conditions or other illnesses. The dogs are trained to respond in different ways if a heart attack or seizure occurs. They might move their owner to a safer place, press an emergency button, or retrieve a phone.

Some dogs seem to be able to predict one of these events and take action before it happens. It is not fully understood how these dogs are aware of this. Several people have reported that they have had fewer seizures since they've had their dogs.

It's easy to see why people who once were afraid to go places because of their illnesses can now lead much more worry-free lives.

Service Dogs (left) and Hearing Dogs (above) wear special jackets or backpacks to show that they are working.

Finding Your Own Cause

Look around you to discover what kinds of organizations exist in your neighborhood. Explore the kinds of projects that help others and improve the community. Maybe there is one just right for you. As you have seen, many wonderful programs began from a simple idea. As more and more people took action and joined in, these programs became bigger and more effective. It is clear that every single person can add something. You never know what kind of difference you can make!

If everybody chipped in even a little bit, what a difference it could make.

Glossary

alert: to notify others that something is happening or about to happen

Assistance Dogs: dogs trained to help people with disabilities

companion: one who lives closely or spends a lot of time with someone else

destruction: the process of ruining or damaging something

ecosystem: a combination of people, animals, and plants, and how they live together in one place

extinction: the condition of a plant or animal species dying off

founders: people who started an organization or group

participate: to take part in an activity

preserved: kept a place safe from harm or destruction

volunteer: someone who gives time and energy to something without getting payment for it

wading: walking through water

wetlands: areas of land where the soil is always wet and moist

Websites

For more about good causes, look at
www.habitat.org
www.everglades.org
www.gophila.com/murals/body.htm
www.pawswithacause.org

Index